THE
GOLDEN
THEME

HOW TO MAKE YOUR WRITING APPEAL TO THE
HIGHEST COMMON DENOMINATOR

BRIAN MCDONALD

TALKING DRUM

THE GOLDEN THEME

Library of Congress Control Number: 2016921319
Cataloging in Publication Data on file with Publisher

Paperback ISBN: 978-0-9985344-1-1
Kindle ISBN: 978-0-9985344-2-8
EPUB ISBN: 978-0-9985344-3-5

Publishing and Production: Concierge Marketing Inc., Omaha, Nebraska

Printed in the United States of America

10 9 8 7 6 5 4 3 2 1

For Mom

A new idea is first condemned as ridiculous and then dismissed as trivial, until finally, it becomes what everybody knows.

—William James

A person experiences life as something separated from the rest—a kind of optical delusion of consciousness. Our task must be to free ourselves from this self-imposed prison, and through compassion, to find the reality of Oneness.

—Albert Einstein

Contents

⋯⋯⋯ ACKNOWLEDGMENTS ⋯⋯⋯

Thanks to Heather for being the one next to me when I came up with the idea for this book. And for *always* being beside me.

And thanks to Bruce Walters who taught me how to see – and how to trust what I saw.

I would also like to list the storytellers whose work has inspired, and guided, me over the years. As I began to compile this list, it kept growing, and I became frightfully aware that when this book sees print I will open it, see this page, and slap my forehead because I have forgotten someone.

So let's just say that this is a partial list of some of the storytellers whose work, and/or life, has pointed me in the direction of the Golden Theme.

They are in no particular order, except for Rod. Everything I know about storytelling started with him:

Rod Serling, Edward Steichen, Billy Wilder, Larry

Gelbart, Paddy Chayefsky, Mark Twain, Chuck Jones, Reginald Rose, Lorraine Hansberry, Charlie Chaplin, George Orwell, John Steinbeck, Gene Rodenberry, Steven Spielberg, Neil Simon, Theodora Lange, George Clayton Johnson, Will Eisner, Gary Ross, Walt Disney, Harvey Bullock, Don Hewitt, Melissa Matheson, Robert Riskin, Stewart Stern, Richard Wright, Martin Ritt, Shirley MacLaine, William Goldman, Albert Hackett, Frances Goodrich, Jonathan Swift, Sydney Pollack, Aesop, Frank Thomas, Ollie Johnston, Jim Henson, Ken Burns, John Ford, Thornton Wilder, Frank Capra, James L. Brooks, Jo Swirling, Ray Bradbury, Fred Moore, Robert Benton, Richard Carter, Alan Alda, Jack Kirby, Steven Zallian, John Houston, Bo Goldman, Leonard Nimoy, Glen Keane, Robert Lewis Stevenson, Harriet Frank Jr., Irving Ravetch, Alex Hailey, Ray Bradbury, Sally Field, Frank Darabont, Alfred Hitchcock, Aaron Ruben, Walter Newman, Lawrence Kasdan, Art Spiegelman, Alvin Sargent, and Billie Holiday.

The next sound you hear will be the slapping of my forehead.

··········· FOREWORD ···········

"As a storyteller, you are a servant of your story, not the master. You must do what it requires, not what you want to do. You must remove your ego from it. Art is not to show people who you are; it is to show people who *they* are."

Brian McDonald

Brian McDonald is one of the world's wisest teachers of the elements that create great storytelling. On this subject, you can trust everything he says, because there is simply no angle or aspect of storytelling – what stories mean and our experience of them – that he has not deeply reflected upon (and from the standpoint of numerous disciplines in the sciences and humanities), then drawn a conclusion that we can take to the bank.

I've had the genuine pleasure of reading both McDonald's *Invisible Ink: A Practical Guide to Building Stories that Resonate* (Believe me, no one dissects with greater subtlety how great films work their magic) and *The Golden Theme: How to Make*

Your Writing Appeal to the Highest Common Denominator, and also watching his wonderful short film "White Face," a fake documentary about what it might be like if clowns were seen as a race of people. If I had not retired last year from teaching classes on literature and the craft of writing at the University of Washington, I would place McDonald's two books before my undergraduate and graduate students as required reading. Though retired, I still plan to tell everyone I know – novelists, short story writers, playwrights, comic book writers, poets, essayists, and screenwriters---about these texts, for in clear, accessible language, with humor and insight and superbly chosen examples, McDonald explains memorably why we, as human beings, need stories for our very day-by-day survival, and why we can discern in the most enduring stories a "Golden Theme" or pattern that is responsible for their power and truth.

For McDonald understands deeply, even profoundly, how it is precisely that –"truth"– which makes stories "vital to our existence." They entertain, yes, but more importantly, he writes, they deliver important information from one generation to the next, and provide an interpretation of our shared experiences as a species. McDonald sees, as all great writers have, that the "uncultivated, feral story" is all around us all the time in the form of anecdotes, gossip, jokes, legends, histories and news stories, and he brilliantly grasps the link between all these forms, how one can easily be transformed into another. Our everyday lives are their "natural habitat."

Put another way, our human minds are hard-wired to shape our experiences into temporal narratives (with beginnings, middles, and ends, and with a conflict that says these events are not pedestrian but instead portray a performer living for high stakes that will speak to *your* life, so pay attention), placing the buzzing chaos of experience into that pattern in order to conjure sense and meaning from it.

Throughout these entertaining and enlightening books, McDonald's reflections are guided by a spiritual maturity and moral lucidity seldom seen in writing about this subject. Whether he is discussing the role played by mirror neurons in our feelings of empathy; the Golden Ratio; 2,500-year old parables like "The Boy Who Cried Wolf"; ayurvedic medicine in the Far East (stories given to patients to help them heal); or a delightful anecdote –"an accidental sociological experiment"– about what happened in 1968 during filming for "Planet of the Apes," his great humanity comes singing off these pages. "I once wrote a story where one of the characters was a slaveholder in the American south," he says. "To find this character's humanity was a challenge for me, as I am a descendent of slaves. But I had to imagine myself in the circumstances of my character's world – I had to find that part of him that was like me."

There is potentially a Hitler in all of us, asserts McDonald, quoting from Mother Teresa, and we must acknowledge these monsters, this darkness within, when we write. "Beware of people who say, 'We are different,'" he counsels us. "Or ones who say, 'We are better.'" For in McDonald's view, there are really no heroes or villains in our literature and films, only human beings acting selfishly or unselfishly, and each one of them has something to teach us. Therefore, he offers this smart advice: "Whenever possible, a storyteller should draw a parallel between the hero's weakness and the villain's. That way the audience can measure the triumph of the hero against the failure of the villain with a direct comparison." And perhaps the most important lesson of all in these stories we've told and retold since we became a distinct group of humanoids between 100,000 and 200,000 years ago (i.e., different from the other 22 species of now extinct humans and pre-humans), is that, "Sacrifice is the ultimate expression of the Golden Theme" underlying our tales of wisdom.

So my recommendation is quite simple:

If you a writer in any genre, read *The Golden Theme*. If you are a non-writing reader who just loves stories, read it. If you are a teacher, share it with your students. And give it to friends, who will thank you for the clarity Brian McDonald so generously brings to our lives.

Charles Johnson
Seattle, 2010

··········· INTRODUCTION ···········

What August Wilson Taught Me about Writing

When I first met August Wilson, I thought, "Here is a guy who can help me understand my craft." I was in a little mall on Seattle's Capitol Hill and I looked over and there he was—a living legend. Mr. Wilson, as I called him then, was reading the paper and standing by himself. He was arguably America's greatest living playwright and undoubtedly the most successful African-American playwright ever. He was internationally respected and almost any dramatist would give anything to be standing where I was at that very moment. I decided that I could not let this opportunity pass by. I approached him nervously and asked if he was August Wilson. He looked at me as if I was going to serve him a subpoena and nodded. I told him what I would witness many people telling him over the years: that he was great and his work was great, etc. He'd heard it all before and was polite but didn't seem to want to talk about himself. August Wilson was not a self-centered man.

Over the next few years, our conversations became longer. He was not just an interesting man; he was an *interested* man. He was much more at home talking to people about themselves than having them gush over him. He even became a fan of my work. (It's still weird to write those words down.) He really liked a film I made called *White Face* and dashed across a busy street to tell me he had seen it and how much he liked it. He went on and on, laughing and reciting lines from the film. From then on he treated me like a peer. I mentioned the story structure class that I teach and he suggested that he should take it. I was blown away. I said, "You have two Pulitzers to my zero! Why would you want to take my class?"

He told me a story about a guy he knew who had once met the great jazz saxophonist John Coltrane. The man sheepishly mentioned to Coltrane that he, too, played the saxophone.

Coltrane's response was: "What can you teach me?"* August wanted to know what I could teach him. In fact, one time I was on my cell phone and August approached and hovered around until I got off the phone. He then asked me for advice on his new play. I told him what I thought and he took notes and listened.

---

* *I did not know it at the time, but August told this story often.*

At first I thought I was part of an exclusive club, being friends with August Wilson. As it turned out, August was there for anyone who was courageous enough to approach. He made friends (real honest-to-goodness friends) with passing homeless people and crack addicts. He knew things about their lives that, when revealed, made these street people into three- dimensional human beings. While most of us would avoid even making eye contact with these people, August Wilson would engage them in conversation.

Of the people August would meet some mornings for coffee, I was the one of the few writers[+]. He was not a cliquish man. Anyone was welcomed into the circle. August Wilson was not the kind of writer who observed life without getting involved in it. He was both an observer and a participant.

When I first met August Wilson, I thought he would teach me about the craft of writing, but he ended up asking me more questions than I ever asked him. What I realize now is that he was teaching me that a writer is always learning and willing to learn. He taught me that living life is the best way to gather material. He taught me that the crack addict on the street may teach you more about life than a college professor. He taught me that you can ask of anyone you meet: What can you teach me? He taught me that if you reach for the humanity in others, you will find it within yourself. All of these things will make you a

+ *Another was Stuart Thayer, author of the book Traveling Showmen about the history of the American circus.*

better writer and a better human being.

It is safe to say that August taught me what I needed to know to write this book.

Thank you, August.

THE GOLDEN THEME

The plurality that we perceive is only an appearance; it is not real.

—Erwin Schrödinger
(physicist who developed quantum mechanics)

I think I have something to share—something about stories and storytelling that has changed me profoundly. And something that may change you.

I am a storyteller, and I have spent my entire life searching for a commonality that links all stories in all forms. The separation and categorization of stories have never made much sense to me. While other story analysts focus on what distinguishes one genre from another (a western from science fiction or a myth from a fairytale, for instance), I see no differences between them.

This idea may be difficult for some readers to comprehend, but I have come to understand that differences in genres are superficial and have little or no bearing on a story's power or truth. *And truth is all that any story worth telling is getting at.* In this regard, what I think I have discovered is the one underlying truth that links all stories.

I know this is a lot to claim, but it hit me one night like a bolt of lightening. This is a simple idea, and when you first hear it you may want to dismiss it out of hand because of its very simplicity. Now, I am a firm believer in the concept that there are no new ideas, but I have not seen this simple idea expressed in just this way anywhere and, believe me, I have looked.

This is not to say that no one has ever said what I am about to tell you. On the contrary, every great artist, poet, spiritual leader, politician, and scientist has said it for millennia. It is just that I have never heard it expressed as a Golden Theme that underlies all stories.

Stories may have individual themes, such as, "there is no honor among thieves" or "slow and steady wins the race." But underneath all stories, no matter what their intentional theme may be, lies another message—a universal message.

How did I come to this understanding of story? Years ago I was walking through a cemetery with a friend and reading headstones, and was struck by a thought. I said to him, "I bet if these people could talk to us they would all say the same thing. They would all have the same thing to tell us."

My friend asked me what this thing was that they would say. I did not know, but I spent the next few years contemplating this question. I think I may know the answer.

Imagine yourself walking through a graveyard. You read the markers. One is the grave of a child, another the grave of a mother. You read the dates, do some quick math, and see that some were older than you and many were younger. Perhaps there are hundreds of headstones in this cemetery. Looking at this sea of graves of those who have lived and died before us, there is only one thing they are trying to tell us, only one lesson to learn.

Think about it. In these graves are people who, like you, wanted to be loved by someone.

They wondered about the nature of life and death. They argued with others about politics and religion. The same sun that warms you warmed them, and at night they looked at the stars with wonder. Like you, they got hungry. Like you, they sometimes thought the customs of others were strange and wrong. Like you, they worried about war with foreign enemies. A cemetery tells us just one thing. And it does not whisper this truth, but shouts it. *The dead tell us this: we are all the same.*

This simple sentence, *we are all the same*, is the Golden Theme that all stories express.

And it is my firm belief that the closer a story comes to illuminating this truth, the more powerful and universal it becomes, and the more people are touched by it.

The pages that follow are my attempt to prove this hypothesis.

Why I Call This the Golden Theme

The few people I have told about this idea of the Golden Theme have asked if the name is derived from the biblical Golden Rule. It is not. That is, not on purpose. I was thinking more about The Golden Ratio.

In art and architecture, there is the ancient mathematical concept of the Golden Mean or Golden Ratio. Its use produces a composition that is pleasing to the eye.

The Great Pyramid of Giza is said to be one of the earliest uses of Divine Proportion, as it is also called, because it was actually thought to be divine. It was said to embody God's perfection. The Greeks used this formula to construct the Parthenon. It was used by painters during the Renaissance and helped them create masterpieces.

In 1854, the German philosopher and mathematician Adolf Zeising wrote:

> [The Golden Ratio is a universal law] in which is

contained the ground-principle of all formative
striving for beauty and completeness in the realms
of both nature and art, and which permeates, as a
paramount spiritual ideal, all structures, forms
and proportions, whether cosmic or individual,
organic or inorganic, acoustic or optical;
which finds its fullest realization, however, in the
human form.

Indeed, Adolf Zeising found this mathematical pattern
of composition throughout the natural world. He found
it in the makeup of plants and in the veins and nerves of
animals, as well as in their skeletons. This includes human
beings.

I wondered if there were such a universal law for story
construction, and after years of contemplation, I hit upon
the Golden Theme.

What is interesting to me now is why I didn't
immediately think of the Golden Rule, as the two are one
and the same.

The Golden Theme is a universal law:
we are all the same.

THE GOLDEN RULE

Do unto others as you would wish them to do onto you.

We were all taught the Golden Rule as children and, if we are honest with ourselves, do not follow it as we should. We Westerners usually learn it as having a biblical origin, but it seems that all cultures have an equivalent concept for their societies.

Christianity	*All things whatsoever ye would that men should do to you, do ye so to them; for this is the law and the prophets.* —Matthew 7:12
Confucianism	*Do not do to others what you would not like yourself. Then there will be no resentment against you, either in the family or in the state.*—Analects 12:2
Buddhism	*Hurt not others in ways that you yourself would find hurtful.*—Udana-Varga 5,1
Hinduism	*This is the sum of duty; do naught onto others what you would not have them do unto you.*—Mahabharata 5,1517

Islam	*No one of you is a believer until he desires for his brother that which he desires for himself.*—Sunnah
Judaism	*What is hateful to you, do not do to your fellowman. This is the entire Law; all the rest is commentary.*—Talmud, Shabbat 3id
Taoism	*Regard your neighbor's gain as your gain, and your neighbor's loss as your own loss.* —Tai Shang Kan Yin P'ien
Zoroastrianism	*That nature alone is good which refrains from doing another whatsoever is not good for itself.*—Dadisten-I-dinik, 94,5

Some philosophers have expressed it this way:

What you would avoid suffering yourself, seek not to impose on others.—Epictetus

Act as if the maxim of thy action were to become by thy will a universal law of nature.—Kant

May I do to others as I would that they should do unto me. —Plato

Do not do to others that which would anger you if others did it to you.—Socrates

Every religion emphasizes human improvement, love, respect for others, sharing other people's suffering. On these lines every religion had more or less the same viewpoint and the same goal.—The Dalai Lama

This is a very old idea that transcends time, culture, and religion. The only conclusion I can draw is that it must be necessary for human survival and peaceful coexistence.

***Virtually every culture has a version of the
Golden Theme.***

WHY HUMANS TELL STORIES

*There have been great societies that did
not use the wheel, but there have been no
societies that did not tell stories.*

—Ursula K. LeGuin

Before we move forward, let's explore the big idea of
why we tell stories. Many, many people have tackled this
subject, but none have answered it to my satisfaction —
and I may not answer the question in a way that suits you,
but I think it may help to at least consider my theory.

A few years ago, I was with some friends at a Mexican

restaurant with outdoor seating. It was a hot day and we ordered blended margaritas. I took one sip and got a blinding headache, commonly known as a "brain freeze." This particular one was like being hit on the head with a sledgehammer.

The next thing I knew I was waking up on the floor surrounded by concerned restaurant patrons. Seeing that I was confused, someone said to me, "It's okay, you just had a seizure."

What? I'd never had a seizure before and had no idea why this would have happened.

Needless to say, I was upset by this news.

I was rushed in an ambulance to the hospital, where they did a series of neurological tests on me while my mother, other family members, and old friends waited to hear whether I had some kind of brain tumor. It was a very scary event.

The doctors finally told me that I was fine. The stupid truth was that I had passed out from the brain freeze. Turns out when your brain is not getting enough blood, your body gets the message to pass out so that you will lie down, allowing blood to flow easily through your body. I was relieved and embarrassed to hear that I had only fainted.

But it made a good story, and I told a few people. Well,

everywhere I went for the next few months people I knew but had not seen in a while greeted me with, "I heard about your brain freeze."

It seemed that this story spread like wildfire. I wondered exactly why people found this story so interesting—so entertaining.

I think it's because buried within the story is survival information. And this survival information is, I believe, the reason we tell stories. We are engaged by stories that contain this kind of information. Not only that, but we also feel compelled to spread this information by repeating the story to others.

In a very real sense, just like living organisms, good stories replicate themselves—they reproduce. And just like living things, the strong survive and the weak die off. A strong story that contains solid survival information can survive for thousands of years.

Imagine a group of early humans at the dawn of time as they forage for grubs and roots.

One of them finds a bush decorated with tasty-looking red berries. Just as he is about to pop one into his mouth, a friend stops him. The friend tells him not to eat those berries because his grandfather told him that once, long ago, many people ate these berries, and after a long, painful illness most of them died.

In a case like that, nature would favor those who listened to stories and learned from them because the ones who did not would die before they could pass on their genes. So the people and the story live on.

We are all descendants of people who understood the importance of stories and inherited this trait, which is why we seek them out and consume them daily.

You may think that my little brain freeze story doesn't have much in the way of survival information. But I guarantee that the next time you have a cold drink and you feel a brain freeze coming on, you will think back on this story and know that your brain is not getting enough blood and that there is no need to panic and rush off to the hospital.

Stories are vital to our existence. Not in any esoteric, abstract way, but in a quite practical way. We could not live without stories.

I know a woman who at one time was a flight attendant and I once asked her if anything scary had ever happened to her on a plane. She went on to tell me that a few people had died on her flights.

Then she told me that once while she was on a flight a young boy was constantly running up and down the aisle, back and forth to the bathroom and annoying the other flight attendants.

My friend was concerned and asked the boy's mother if he was okay. The mother said that she thought so. My friend then noticed that the boy's lower lip was swollen and asked about it.

The mother said that she didn't know what it was and thought that maybe the boy had been bitten by a bug or something.

It was then that my friend was reminded of a story that her parents had told her about her father. Turns out her father has a severe fish allergy, and once his lip swelled as a reaction. He was rushed to the emergency room where he was treated.

My friend asked the boy's mother if the boy was allergic to fish. The woman did not know. But my friend checked the flight's menu and saw that they had served a salad with shrimp, and suspected this was an allergic reaction.

The plane had a direct line to the Mayo Clinic, so my friend called and they confirmed her suspicions and instructed her on what to do. When the plane landed, there was a medical team waiting. It turns out the boy might have gotten very ill or even died if my friend had not remembered this story.

This is exactly how we use stories every day. When my friend heard this story about her father, she did not consciously file it away to be pulled out just when she needed it. But there it was, easily retrieved, when she did need it. This is story in its natural habitat.

As long as there have been people, and wherever there are people, they have told stories.

If this were not essential to our survival, there would surely be people without stories. But there are none in the history of the world.

Stories are a way to get the benefit of someone else's experience without having to have the experience oneself. For example on January 15, 2009, shortly after take-off, US Airways Flight 1549 piloted by Capt. Chesley "Sully" Sullenberger was struck by a flock of geese and had to make an emergency landing on the Hudson River in New York. This incident became known as "Miracle on the Hudson" and Sully became a hero.

The day of this famous landing I was watching MSNBC's Keith Olbermann show, which reported the breaking news. By phone, Mr. Olbermann spoke with Denny Fitch, the pilot of another famed crash landing, to get an expert opinion on the incident.

Fitch said that he thought that Sully was the perfect pilot to handle such an emergency because he had been an accident investigator for the Nation Transportation Safety Board (NTSB). He had plenty of stories in his head of emergency situations that were handled poorly and knew how to avoid the mistakes of these other pilots.

If you think about it this is the only reason to have the NTSB. Why investigate accidents at all? It can't help the victims of the crash. But it may help others in the future. So we investigate to help others who might one day face the same, or a similar, set of circumstances.

Knowing these stories help pilots and airlines reduce the number of tragic accidents.

Sully had more of these stories in his head than most pilots. This was the equivalent of having more flight experience.

In fact, Fitch said something I found fascinating. He told Keith Olbermann that most pilots "go to school every day." He said they engage in what is called "hangar flying." Hangar flying, as he described it, is when pilots are on the ground exchanging stories of being in hairy situations. He said that this was a way for them to learn from what others had gone through. It was a way to go to school on someone else's tuition, he said.

Hangar flying is a perfect example of how we use stories every day. Most of us are just not as aware as the pilots that we are doing it.

When I was a kid, in about 5th or 6th grade, there was a steep hill in our neighborhood that was used for sledding whenever there was enough snow. Every new kid was told a particular story upon his arrival. It was about a boy, a generation or so before us, who had been sledding when he accidentally crashed into a utility pole one his way down the hill.

The boy had the wind knocked out of him, but felt more or less okay. He did go home though, and laid down for a nap. He never woke up. He had broken a rib and punctured an internal organ.

In hearing that story, we all learned both to be careful going down the hill, and that if we did have an accident, to be sure we weren't more hurt than we first thought.

I remember passing this story along after I had heard it, the same as it was passed to me.

My guess is it's still being told. Even as children we could not help but pass along survival information in the form of a story. We had no idea we were doing so, but we did it just the same.

We all do as the neighborhood kids did on top of that snowy hill—we tell stories because we find them interesting for some reason and can't help but to share them.

The story of the Titanic has many lessons, but one of them is that there ought to be enough lifeboats for everyone onboard a ship. How many lives has this saved?

We have all heard a story about someone whose life was

saved because she was wearing her seatbelt. There were enough stories of horrific deaths before seatbelts that eventually it became the law that all cars have them and that we wear them.

Because stories contain valuable survival information, we are ravenous consumers of stories and seek them out daily. You might get your daily requirement of story nourishment by reading the news, reading a book, listening to the radio, or gossiping and talking with co-workers and friends. Chances are you did one or more of these things today. In fact, I have told a few stories to you since you started reading this. We cannot escape them, nor can we live without them.

When I was a young child, a family friend lost the use of his legs when he was struck by a car while opening his car door without looking behind him.

You will not be able to stop yourself from remembering this story whenever you exit a car on the side of traffic. That story gives us survival information, so we tuck it away until we need it. We have an endless number of such stories in our heads.

Not all stories are about saving one's physical life; some are about things like getting along in a society, such as "The Boy Who Cried Wolf." Its lesson is: if you are known to be a liar, you will not be believed even when you tell the truth. Understanding this will help one to be a trusted member of society, which is always good for one's survival. "The Boy Who Cried Wolf" is over 2,500 years old. It must have a powerful nutrient to have remained alive for so long.

Still another kind of story teaches us to have the proper mental attitude to succeed in life.

One such story is "The Tortoise and the Hare." The lesson there is: slow and steady wins the race. It is a story that illustrates the value of perseverance.

One of my favorite stories is the Zen parable "The Blind Men and the Elephant." In this story, six blind men came upon an elephant. They had never seen an elephant so they all explored the animal with their hands.

The first man felt the broad side of the elephant and told the others that an elephant is much like a wall. The second man felt the tusk and said, "No, the elephant is round and smooth and sharp." The third man approached the animal, found the trunk, and said that an elephant was "just like a snake." The fourth blind man reached out and grabbed a leg and said, "The elephant is like a tree." The fifth man touched the ear and said, "Even the blindest man can tell that what this animal resembles is a fan!" The sixth happened to grasp the tail and proclaimed that his friends were all wrong. "The elephant is very much like a rope," he said.

The men continued to argue, each holding to his own opinion, even though they all had a piece of the truth.

This story tells us that we may each have a part of the truth and that we would do well to listen to one another to get a clearer picture of things. Think of how many disputes, both large and small, could be avoided if we all heeded the lesson of this story.

Some of you are thinking that some stories exist strictly for entertainment and have no survival information. Think about it this way: is food for tasting good? Is that its sole purpose?

No. Food is what we use for fuel. We absorb valuable nutrients from the consumption of food.

Yes, food can taste good and stories can be entertaining, but this is not why we have a need to consume them.

I believe that stories without a point are on par with eating poison. It is like eating a diet of fast food. It may taste good, but it is, in fact, slowly killing you. It is no coincidence that bad stories have been called "junk food" and "bubble gum"—flavor without nutrition.

But remember: good food does not need to be tasteless, and good stories do not need to be pointless.

We need stories to live.

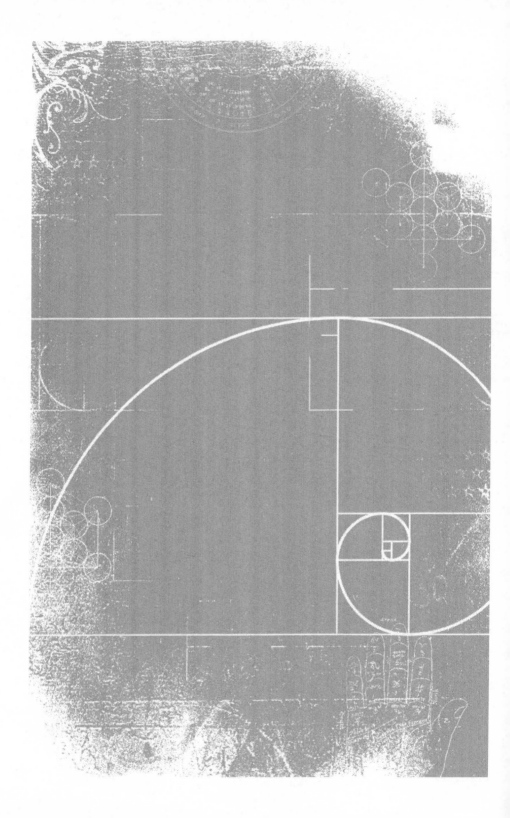

······ WHY STORIES NEED CONFLICT ······

Smooth seas make poor sailors.

– Nautical proverb

Most writing teachers will tell you that stories need conflict, that this is what makes stories interesting. Journalists have a saying: "If it bleeds, it leads," meaning that violence will get people to read your paper or watch your broadcast. Why?

Again, it is all about survival. One does not need to know how to survive when things are going well, only when they are not.

A few months ago, a young woman who lived on my block was brutally stabbed to death outside her apartment building. Needless to say, this was upsetting to everyone in the city, but particularly in the neighborhood where the killing took place.

I, my girlfriend, everyone, wanted to know the details. Why? Survival. They hadn't caught the man who did this. So we all wanted to know if he was still in the area. What did he look like? Did anyone see him? Did he know her? Was it random?

Did we want these details because we were morbid? No, it's because it was vital for our survival to know.

Turns out the killing was random. The man was a resident of a nearby halfway house for mentally disturbed offenders. Also a valuable detail.

In late December 2007, there was a tiger attack at the San Francisco Zoo, and for the next week or so the story was one of the top Internet searches. This is because this story gets right to the heart of survival. One of the most primal concerns of all animals, including human beings, is to find food or not to become food. This fear of being eaten is an ancient fear that resides deep in our reptilian brain.

One of our other top concerns is the protection of our young. This is survival in a bigger sense; this is about the survival of the species. Therefore, people had more than a passing interest in just how this tiger got loose. After all, zoos are mostly visited by parents and children. The details of the story do, in fact, tell us how we can avoid such a fate. Or, at the very least, decrease the likelihood of such a violent end.

According to an Associated Press story about the incident, the victims were intoxicated and provoked the tiger by standing atop the animal's enclosure and yelling at the cat. The San Francisco Times reported that police believed that the tiger may have been agitated by the taunts of the young men involved.

It was also reported that authorities believe the tiger had leaped or climbed out of its enclosure because it had a wall 4 feet shorter than the recommended minimum.

It was also found that the men were intoxicated not just on alcohol but marijuana as well.

Is there any survival information contained in this story? I would say so. You will never be able to see a tiger at the zoo without this story coming to mind.

Compelling stories contain conflict because conflict is always about the struggle to survive. You may think that interpersonal conflicts are not about survival because they are not about being eaten, but understanding how to get along with others can be a useful survival skill.

What about love stories? At their core, love stories are either about learning to be a person who is worthy of love, or about that most primal of urges, propagation of the species—survival.

Hollywood often exploits our craving for stories with survival information by promising a lot of conflict in the film trailers. But it is almost always conflict without purpose. It is exploitation. But we are fooled again and again because we crave the information much the same way we crave sugar.

Evolutionary biologists will tell you that we crave sugar because sweet things, such as fruit, were good for our ancestors. The problem is that now we can refine sugar so that there are no nutrients left and it is, in fact, poison to us. We have plenty of information telling us how bad sugar is for us.

We know sugar causes things like obesity and diabetes, but this doesn't stop us from craving it. Bad stories that promise nutrition but don't deliver go against everything stories are for.

Stories must contain conflict because they teach us to survive life's difficulties.

STORIES IN THEIR NATURAL HABITAT

You can observe a lot just by watching.

– Yogi Berra

What is a story? A story is the telling or retelling of events. By that definition, here is a list of what might be considered stories:

Anecdotes

Gossip

Jokes

Myths

Legends

Urban legends

Parables

Histories

News stories

Biographies

I'm not sure how many categories and subcategories stories can be divided into, but I'm sure it's a pretty big number. Most people who study storytelling limit themselves to just one category. But almost none study story in its natural form—the uncultivated, feral story. Few study the everyday uses of story by people who do not consider themselves writers. And if they do study this type of storytelling, they fail to connect it to the other forms, and to place them all under the umbrella of storytelling.

We can learn everything we need to know about how a story is constructed and why we tell them by observing them in their natural habitat—plain ol' human speech.

Just as the study of Latin can help one understand the languages and words derived from that parent, or root, form, stories can be better understood by looking at their parent form. The parent form of story contains within it every other form.

This will be difficult for some to swallow because we have a bias for the written word.

The word "illiterate" not only means one is unable to read and write, but also that one is unintelligent. In our society, "book smart" is smart. And it is because of this, I believe, that spoken stories are not given the same respect as those written down.

Let's not forget that there were preliterate cultures that did just fine without written language for a very long time. But not one without stories.

Storytelling is an innate human trait, but writing is a human invention that, while useful, is not necessary for survival. So studying stories in written form rather than spoken form is once removed from the source. The spoken story is the seed that the vast tree of story, with its many branches, has grown from. "Mighty oaks from tiny acorns grow," as the saying goes.

For instance, imagine ancient times wherein a few tribesmen go on a hunting trip. They return, having had a successful kill. But one of the men was badly hurt on the hunt. The men recount the story—this is journalism. They infuse the telling with details to convey the emotions they felt—now it's an adventure story. Some of the men play the parts of animals and hunters as the story is told—theater. They tell how the injured man was hurt doing something he should not have—a teaching story. In years to come, the same story becomes history and legend.

This is a hypothetical tale meant to illustrate how one simple story can hold many forms within it. I believe that our separation of story forms is artificial and that there is almost no difference between one and another. Even the idea of fiction and nonfiction is artificial in the world of storytelling.

Is "The Boy Who Cried Wolf" fact or fiction? You may think this is an easy question to answer—*of course it is a work of fiction; this shepherd boy probably never lived and these incidents never occurred.* You are more than likely correct—these things never happened.

But if one looks at it another way, this is a true story. It is true because, in the broader sense, it happens all the time. People often lie again and again, then find that they are not believed even when they speak the truth. From a storyteller's point of view, it is a true story because it contains a Truth. It contains vital survival information. All stories worth telling are true stories. No matter how unbelievable the facts of a story may be, they can still contain vital information.

On December 26, 2004, there was an earthquake with a magnitude of between 9.1 and 9.3 in the Indian Ocean that caused devastating tsunamis that killed around 225,000 people in eleven countries. The hardest hit were Indonesia, Sri Lanka, India, and Thailand.

But the Moken people, who live on the coasts of Thailand and Burma, suffered no deaths at all because they believed in an ancient legend. A story saved their lives. When the ocean receded and a small wave rolled in, the Moken people knew that it meant a tsunami was coming, and they headed for higher ground.

Their legend says that there will be seven waves before the big wave comes—the wave that eats people. It's called the *Laboon* and it is caused by the angry spirits of the ancestors.

When the spirit of the sea becomes hungry and wants to taste people again, it sends a wave to swallow them up. The water destroys the earth to make it clean again.

Is the story that these people believe true? It was true enough to save them. The facts of the story matter little. Sadly, there are people who did not survive who would have known that earthquakes, not angry spirits, cause tidal waves. But this fact did not save them.

In Africa, they used to tell the story of a black slave-catcher who helped the English capture his own countrymen and sell them into a life of slavery. One night, after a particularly good catch, the black slave-catcher was celebrating with the English and they all got drunk on rum. The black man passed out, and when he awoke the next day, he found himself in the belly of a slave ship chained to the very people he helped enslave.

This is a cautionary tale that teaches its listener that there is a price to be paid for betrayal.

These are stories in their natural habitat. It is how we all use stories. I was recently at a gathering with friends because our friend Heidi and her three-year-old daughter Laila were visiting from California. Somehow the subject of seatbelts came up, and Heidi said Laila would reprimand anyone who isn't wearing a seatbelt because she knows the story of when mommy was a little girl and fell out of the car.

A few years ago two teens in a nearby town died while drag racing. The television news reported on the tragic event and interviewed people who were there to see the wreckage. Many of the people were mothers with their teenage boys. They wanted to show them what could happen to them if they were foolish. That two kids were racing and were killed is a simple story, but it contains all-important survival information.

There is a pattern of older people telling stories to younger ones. This is because older people are a collection of experiences, and they pass on these experiences though story so that younger people can benefit.

These are stories in their natural habitat, and you can learn all you need to know about creating stories if you observe the ones around you every day, in virtually every conversation you have or overhear.

Because we live in a culture with a written word bias, we confuse the importance of a story with the wordsmithing—the language used. But all good stories transcend language, culture, and time.

The beauty of a Shakespeare play is only partially in the language, but it is the language that we tend to praise most. What is even more important is the humanity expressed in his plays.

These things are universal, whereas mere language is not, beautiful though it may be.

Good stories work because no matter where we live or when we live, we are all the same.

Everything one wants to know about storytelling can be learned just by listening to people tell stories in everyday lives.

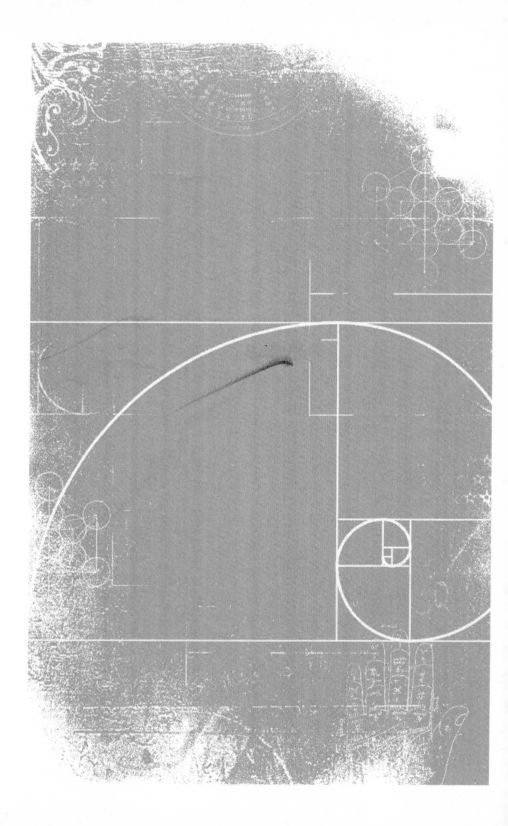

·········· How Stories Work ··········

The great gift of human beings is that we have the power of empathy.

–Meryl Streep

Stories could not work if the Golden Theme were not true. It is our ability to imagine ourselves in story circumstances and to empathize that makes stories work.

During the time of American slavery, the enslaved were not allowed to gather for fear that they might plot against their masters. They could, however, meet for worship. One of the early justifications for slavery was that the heathens were being converted to Christianity, so the slaves were prohibited from practicing their native religions.

The slaves felt a particular affinity for the Biblical story of Moses: the story of an ancient enslaved people to whom God sent a savior to set them free and lead them to a promised land of milk and honey.

These slaves were not Jewish, nor did they live in ancient Egypt. These people were separated by culture, ethnicity, and time, and yet the story of Moses gave the hopeless hope.

Even one hundred years after American slavery, Martin Luther King Jr. cast himself as a Moses-like figure during his famous Mountaintop speech made on the eve of his death:

> Like anybody, I would like to live a long life.
> Longevity has its place. But I'm not concerned
> about that now. I just want to do God's will. And
> He's allowed me to go up to the mountain.
> And I've looked over. And I've seen the Promised
> Land. I may not get there with you. But I
> want you to know tonight, that we,
> as a people will get to the Promised Land.

Slaves are slaves no matter when or where they live. We all want control over our own lives. Our ability to empathize with people we have never met or, as is the case in some stories, never even existed, is proof of the Golden Theme.

Storytellers and other artists have known this for millennia, but now science is finding proof of this as well. Even our own biology tells us this is so because, as it turns out, we are hardwired to feel what others are feeling.

Italian neuroscientists in Parma, Italy, led by Giacomo Rizzolatti have discovered something dubbed "mirror neurons." They observed that cells in monkeys' brains were activated when the monkeys made movements, but what the researchers found, quite by accident, was that the same neurons were activated when the monkeys watched others make movements. The monkeys' brains didn't know the difference between doing a thing and watching that same thing.

Further research has found that humans have even more highly evolved mirror neurons than monkeys. So our brains do not understand the difference between doing and watching.

I am frightened of getting injections; I would guess more frightened than most of you. Trust me.

But I have noticed that when I'm sitting in a movie theater and someone on screen gets an injection, everyone in the audience winces along with me. That's because their mirror neurons are working to produce empathy.

I'll even bet that some of you winced just reading about injections, didn't you? This is how stories work on us. As far as our brains are concerned, we are having the experience in the story.

"Mirror neurons allow us to grasp the minds of others not through conceptual reasoning but through direct simulation. By feeling, not by thinking," said Dr. Rizzolatti in the January 10, 2006, edition of the *New York Times*.

Scientists believe that understanding the actions and feelings of others has helped human beings survive. Some speculate that autism, a brain disorder that impairs social interaction and communication, may be a result of a broken mirror system.

If this is true, it is easy to see just how important it is that we think what others think and feel what others feel. Otherwise survival is much more difficult.

When we listen to another's story we are all 'hanger flying', as pilot Denny Fitch called it. We all go to school on 'someone else's tuition' every time we hear a story.

We can learn the lesson of a story because as far as our brains are concerned, it has actually happened to us.

Stories as Medicine

We spend all our life trying to be less lonesome. One of our ancient methods is to tell a story begging the listener to say—and to feel—'Yes, that's the way it is, or at least that's the way I feel it. You're not as alone as you thought.'

—John Steinbeck

Ayurvedic medicine is one of the oldest forms of healing in the world and is still practiced in India, Sri Lanka, and Nepal. Among other methods of healing, practitioners also use stories to help their patients by giving the patient a story to contemplate. Through this story, the patient learns from the hero's failures and victories how to deal with and resolve his or her own problem.

In the West, we have used blues music for healing. The blues often tell a story of some tragic event, but people who listen to blues music say that it makes them feel good. Why? Because the blues let us know that others share our troubles—that we are not alone in our suffering. This is medicinal for us.

Unhappy teenagers have been known to listen to music that validates their feelings of depression. It helps them know that they may be lonely, but that they are not alone.

The knowledge that others have had the same woes can change lives. In twelve-step programs such as Alcoholics Anonymous, people do little more than share stories, and yet they have a substantial recovery rate. The knowledge that we are not alone and that others are like us is as good as any drug.

PBS ran a documentary called *The Undertaking* on an episode of its show *Frontline*. It was an amazing documentary from the perspective of an undertaker on the subject of death and dying.

In the film, a young couple has a terminally ill child. The mother tells a story about how she goes to the cemetery to read the old headstones from the pioneer days. There she sees the markers of women who lost children, sometimes more than one or two, and yet they lived on, these women. They went through the pain of losing children and still they survived.

The young mother, her sick child cradled on her lap, said she was comforted by these stories and that she knew she would—and could—go on after her own child's death because other women had.

Sometimes the knowledge that others have survived is the survival information people need from a story. Like the Moses story for the slaves, it can help us live one more day, and one more day, until finally we have lived through the ordeal.

Letting people know they are not alone in their suffering is one of the primary responsibilities of a storyteller. We human beings are always looking for connections. This is why it is so important to understand the Golden Theme.

When human beings want to find some connection with others, sometimes those connections are superficial, as in, "You like that band, too!" And sometimes the connections are profound: "I had a little brother who died, too." But we are compelled to seek them out.

According to the book *Cell Talk* by John E. Upledger, even like cells seek each other. "It has been seen in the laboratory that different types of cells, when mixed in a culture, will segregate into clusters." It is deep within us to find similarities.

I have a friend who is a veteran of World War II and recently joined a support group of veterans. Since he has been going there and talking to others who understand the horrors of war, in a way that most of us do not, he has more vigor. He appears younger, more vibrant and altogether in much better spirits. This is just from sharing stories with like-minded souls. He still has the memories of the horrific past. They have not gone away, and yet somehow he is better.

In 1968, a film called *Planet of the Apes* was released. In the story, an astronaut has landed on a planet populated by apes that possess a humanlike intelligence. During the making of this film, an accidental sociological experiment took place.

In the film, there were three kinds of apes—orangutans, gorillas, and chimpanzees. Each type of ape occupied a different level in a strict caste system. This was before the days of computer graphics, and actors in makeup played the apes. The makeup was very complicated and required several hours to apply. This meant that the actors could not remove their makeup for lunch and had to eat wearing their masks.

Some of these actors had known each other for years. But when it came time to eat, they did not eat with their friends; chimps ate with chimps, orangutans ate with orangutans, and gorillas ate with gorillas.

We seek out commonalties and we are often fooled by a cosmetic kinship, but we have an altogether deeper feeling when we connect with someone emotionally.

This is why we go to events where we can share a common experience. There is nothing like sitting in a darkened theater or concert hall when everyone around us is feeling the same thing at the same time—when our emotions are in sync. You can almost feel an electrical charge in the air. It is an exhilarating feeling. It is the feeling we get when we are aware that we are all the same. That feeling is a powerful medicine.

By looking at AA and other twelve-step programs, we can see that stories can be a tool for healing.

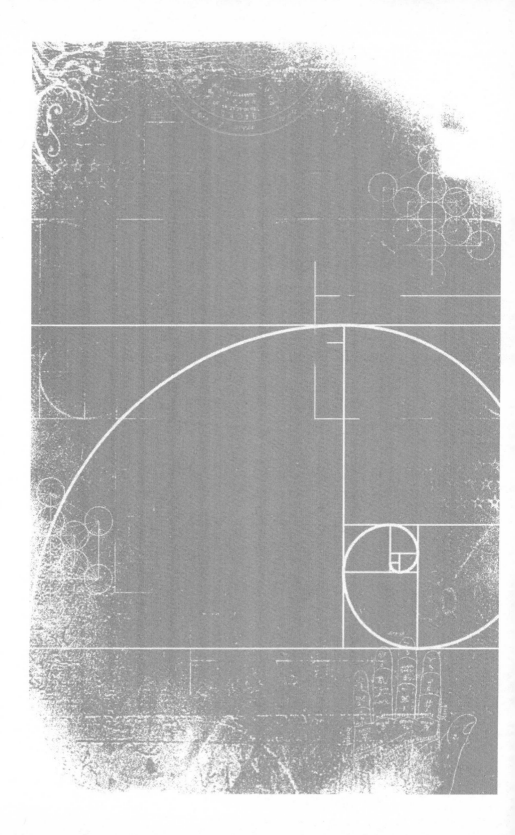

Animal Tales and the
Golden Theme

....

*All animals are equal but some animals are
more equal than others.*

—George Orwell, Animal Farm

People have used animals in storytelling for all of
human history. The ancient Greeks believed that by
observing the way a beehive was organized and following
that model, you could have a perfect society. Many tribal
peoples believe that one has an animal spirit guide and by
following that animal's lead, one might have an easier time

in life. Tribal people also believe that we have an animal side to our natures—what Carl Jung calls a "bush soul." So, not only do we see ourselves in animals, but also we see the animal within ourselves.

But why do we use animals in stories practically? Often this is an easier way to illustrate the Golden Theme because it is a way to look at ourselves with a little distance.

One of my favorite storytellers, Aesop, used animal stories to illuminate the nature of human beings. If the story of "The Tortoise and the Hare" were merely what the title suggests, few would remember the story. No, this is a story about people—people "dressed" for the story like a tortoise and a hare—but people nonetheless.

In the American South, during the time of slavery, slaves told stories of the clever Brer (Brother) Rabbit. These were not stories of rabbits, foxes, and bears, but stories about people designed to help them survive their cruel circumstances, stories about slaves outwitting their masters to get what they wanted and needed.

George Orwell's book *Animal Farm* uses that distance to reveal how people in power can abuse that power. Art Spiegelman's brilliant graphic novel *Maus* uses cats as Nazis and mice as Jews to give the reader just enough emotional distance to see a Holocaust story through fresh eyes.

Less seriously, Daffy Duck provides the distance

necessary to notice our greedy natures and laugh at ourselves and how we sometimes deny the truth of the Golden Theme.

But it isn't only animals that provide this distance; it can be time or the world itself that provides the distance. Many stories begin, "Long ago in a far away land…." Why? So that we are not confused by the specifics—everything is stripped away but the truth. This makes stories more universal and timeless. Good stories are eternal because the truth can't tell time.

This, I believe, is why fantasy stories have always been popular. Fantasy is not mere escapism, as is so often stated, but just the opposite. It is a way of talking about reality— of telling the truth.

One of my storytelling heroes is Rod Serling, creator of the classic television show *The Twilight Zone*. Fed up with restrictions enforced on him by networks and advertisers, Mr. Serling stopped writing the prestigious teleplays for live television for which he was famous.

When he announced that he would be doing a fantasy show, many thought he had given up on doing "serious work" for television. Mr. Serling knew something the executives didn't. "I knew I could have Martians say things that Democrats and Republicans couldn't," he said.

He wrote fantastical stories about real human issues

without any flack from advertisers and these fantasies have outlasted his "serious" work to become classics.

Your stories can take place in the past, future, on another world, or have talking animals in them, but as long as they express the Golden Theme they will speak to people. In fact, they may even speak the truth more clearly than any so-called "true story."

Using animals or some other device gives an audience distance from a story, allowing them to focus on the story's point.

HUMAN RIGHTS AND
THE GOLDEN THEME

I happen to think that the singular evil of our time is prejudice. It is from this evil that all other evils grow and multiply.

—Rod Serling

Simply put, prejudice is ignorance or willing denial that we are all the same. When we humans find ourselves in a conflict with one another, one of the first things we do is focus on our differences. The differences themselves don't matter—they can be anything:

Height

Eye shape

Skin color

Language or manner of speech

Dress

Religion

Technological advancement

Body type

Food

Hair texture

Economic class

Gender

Sexual orientation

Music

Cultural customs

System of government

History

Level of education

These are just a few; I'm sure that you could think of more. These are superficial differences that sometimes blind us from seeing the deeper truth of our sameness. The truth is that when we fight wars because of these differences we all grieve our dead.

Below is a list of epithets we use to deny the idea that we are all the same:

Jewish people

Hymie

Kike

Shyster

Shylock

Christ killer

Jew boy

People of African descent

Alligator bait

Ape

Coon

Jigaboo

Jungle bunny

Kaffir

Macaca

Nigger

Sambo

Tar baby

Thicklips

Smoked Irish

East Asian descent

Charlie

Chee-chee

Chinaman

Chink

Gook

People of Italian descent

Dago

Ginzo

Goombah

Greaseball

Guinea

Wog

Wop

People of Irish descent

Bog Irish

Dogan

Mick

Paddy

Piker

West Brit

White nigger

Whigger

Homosexual people

Fag

Faggot

Nance

Queer

Fairy

Pansy

Queen

We use these terms to dehumanize one another, but the best among us will always stand up and say that we are all the same.

Mahatma Gandhi stood up to the British government, demanding that the people of India be treated with respect and given their independence. What else was he saying but that we are all the same?

In 1955, Rosa Parks, an African-American woman, broke Montgomery, Alabama, law when she refused to give up her bus seat to a white man. What else was she saying but that we are all the same?

When America declared independence from British rule, the founders started with these words: "We hold these truths to be self-evident: That all men are created equal; that they are endowed by their Creator with certain unalienable rights; that among these are life, liberty, and the pursuit of happiness...."

Even though the Declaration of Independence left out women, Native Americans, and slaves, the spirit of the document is clear—we are all the same.

The Danish people take much pride in the story of King Christian X, who defied the Nazis when they occupied his country. As the story goes, the Nazis gave an order that all Danish Jews were to wear yellow stars identifying themselves as Jews.

King Christian proclaimed, "Then we are all Jews," and wore a star himself—as did all Danish people.

In my research I found that this did not happen. No such order was given in Denmark.

But whether this story is true or not has no bearing on its power. This story is told and retold and because it affirms that the Danish people and their leader recognized the humanity of others.

We will always take pride in such stories and pass them along because whether they are factual or not, they have at their core the great truth that we are all the same.

Across culture and across time we view those who understand the Golden Theme as heroes and those who do not as villains.

Mother Teresa, who spent her life caring for the dying and the poor, said she dedicated herself to doing so "on the day I discovered I had a Hitler inside me." Mother Teresa's life is the pure expression of the Golden Theme. She was able to see herself in others, and so could not turn away from those in need.

This is how we judge heroes, through their expression of the Golden Theme, through their actions. You can hear it in the way we speak when we describe a good person as the kind of person who would give you the shirt off his back—self-sacrifice. In 1994, there was genocide in Rwanda (genocide is a denial of the Golden Theme). The President of Rwanda had died in a plane crash and soon the government called for the people of the Hutu tribe to kill the people of another tribe, the Tutsis.

In her book *Left to Tell*, a young Tutsi woman named Immaculée Ilibagiza, tells how she survived this Rwandan holocaust because she was hidden, along with seven other women, in a tiny bathroom for ninety days. A pastor, who was a Hutu, hid them. During this time, the women and the pastor were in grave danger. The killing outside was brutal: people were being hacked to death with machetes. The pastor's house was searched several times, but the women were not found. This pastor understood the Golden Theme enough to know that anyone else's life was as precious as his own.

Throughout history every great person, movement, or cause has evoked the Golden Theme and operates in the world with it as a guiding principle, saying, "We are all the same," or "We are in this together."

On the other hand, we may say of a bad person that he thinks only of himself—selfishness. Beware of people who say, "We are different." Or ones who say, "We are better."

These have always been, and will always be, the villains. This is as true in the world of stories as it is in life.

The villain of the 20th century, Adolph Hitler, said, "Was there any form of filth or profligacy, particularly in cultural life, without at least one Jew involved in it? If you cut even cautiously into such an abscess, you found, like a maggot in a rotting body, often dazzled by the sudden light—a kike!"

This is a man who believed that he, and those with his history, were better than others. He thought only of himself, which is the overriding trait of villainy.

The seven deadly sins are aspects of self-centered behavior:

Pride

Envy

Anger

Sloth

Greed

Gluttony

Lust

Forget that this list has its origins in the Catholic religion. I suspect it goes back much further than that. These characteristics in people would make it very hard to function within a society, and I imagine that all people at every time and in every culture have had some version of this list.

The dragon, the European dragon, is a monster who sits on a pile of gold it does not need—greed. Monsters in stories embody one or more aspects of this list.

The evil queen in the story of Snow White was so concerned with being the most beautiful that she was willing to kill Snow White. She was consumed with vanity.

In history, King Henry VIII ruled over England but was ruled by his ravenous appetites

for food, power, and women. He was possessed by gluttony.

Villains will always exhibit selfish behavior that is in direct opposition to the Golden Theme. This yardstick for good and evil is universal. Bad people will always put their wants and needs first and almost never consider the needs of others. And good people will put the lives of others on a par with their own. Great people put the lives of others before their own.

Another quote from Hitler: "Humanitarianism is the expression of stupidity and cowardice."

This is not the quote of a good person and we all know it, even if we did not know who he was.

On the other hand, here is a quote from Albert Schweitzer, a German doctor who spent his life running a hospital in Gabon, Africa, early in the 20th century: "Humanitarianism consists in never sacrificing a human being to a purpose."

The words and actions of these two people show us who was the hero and who was the villain.

We use the Golden Theme in life to determine who is good and who is not.

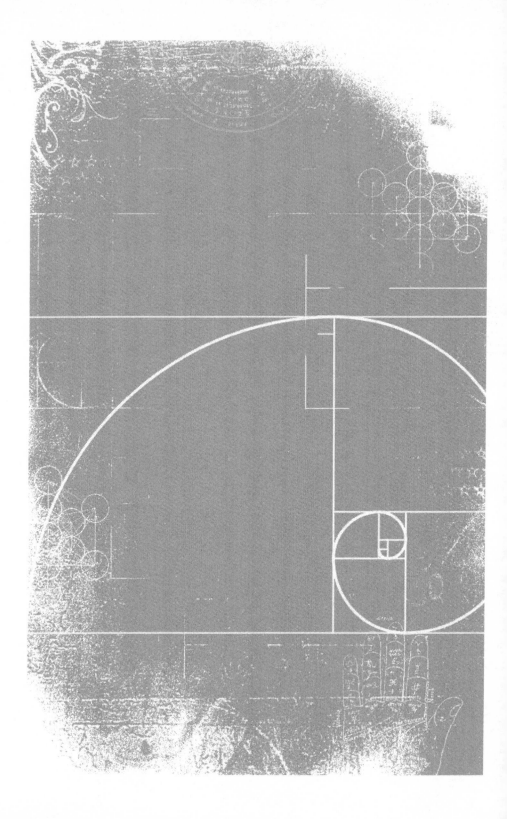

THE HITLER IN YOU

Let us strive to be fully human and there will be no longer a place for evil.

—Confucius

Let's revisit Mother Teresa's quote, "on the day I discovered I had a Hitler inside me." This is a profound understanding of the Golden Theme, to be able to see the monster in oneself. In order to be good storytellers, we must recognize that monsters are nothing but the worst versions of ourselves. Monsters in both the story world and the living world are only manifestations of us.

This is a hard pill to swallow because we do not want to

see the monster in us, but it is always there waiting for a moment to break free.

I once wrote a story where one of the characters was a slaveholder in the American south.

To find this character's humanity was a challenge for me, as I am a descendant of slaves. But I had to imagine myself in the circumstances of my character's world—I had to find the part of him that was like me. I had to understand that the people of the past were made of the same flesh and bone and had all the same feelings and thoughts. In short, they were just like me.

These people who were slaveholders grew up in a world where this was the system. They would usually be given a slave playmate as a child, so that both slave and future master knew their places in society. Now imagine that to give up this system would mean abject poverty for you. Put it in today's terms, would you give up all you own if it meant that factories around the world would stop using child labor? Would you do that if it meant you would lose everything?

Most of us would not.

Let's look at the violence of the slave system. This was a system of fear. Imagine that your life was the only thing that stood between you and the freedom of one hundred and fifty men, women, and children.

I remember when I was a child and my mother told me for the first time that black people were once slaves. This is a hard thing for a child to grasp. My mother explained it by saying that not only did it mean working for free, but that it also meant that she, my brother, my sister, or I could be sold away from each other—that one day one of us might go away forever. That I understood.

Imagine that you were a slaveholder and had broken up families. How well would you sleep knowing that there were grieving mothers and angry fathers just outside your door?

Imagine their hatred for you.

Even though you deny the Golden Theme, you know it to be true. It is the only way to imagine how your slaves would feel. You know on some level that they are just like you. You know that what hurts you hurts them. But you suppress it because it is too much to bear.

George Washington freed his slaves in his will, effective upon the death of his wife Martha. The idea that she was the sole reason these people were still slaves made her fear for her life. She freed the slaves herself while she lived. She knew how she would feel in the same situation as the people she owned.

It was this kind of fear that made people violent and cruel to their slaves. It was the only way to control so many people. Both slave and slaveholder lived in constant fear. No matter what it looked like, both were slaves.

Imagine that you were born into that world instead of ours. Imagine being told from your earliest years that this was the way it was and should be. Imagine who this would make you. Find the thing that would make you behave as the cruelest of slaveholders and you will have found his humanity and your own. Remember, these were just people. Just like you.

This is when it becomes a challenge to believe in the Golden Theme: when you must confront the monster inside, but it is there.

Playwright August Wilson said, "To live it [life] as an artist is to be willing to face the deepest parts of yourself. To wrestle with your demons until your spirit becomes larger and larger and your demons smaller and smaller."

To that end, please answer this list of questions as honestly as possible:

> Have you ever, as a child or adult, been cruel to anyone?
>
> Have you ever, as a child or adult, been selfish?
>
> Have you ever, as a child or adult, not stood up for something you know is right?

Have you ever, as a child or adult, gone with the crowd to be accepted?

Have you ever, as a child or adult, believed yourself to be better in some way than those around you?

Have you ever, as a child or adult, lied about yourself to impress others?

Have you ever been driven by an obsession or addiction of any kind?

Have you ever, as a child or adult, lied to yourself?

Have you ever, as a child or adult, let your fear control you?

Do you harbor a secret shame?

Have you ever, as a child or adult, let any negative emotions or attitudes, such as depression, anger, jealousy, fear, or arrogance, get the best of you?

Have you ever, as a child or adult, ignored the suffering of others?

Have you ever, as a child or adult, been envious of someone else's abilities, looks, money, or status?

Have you ever, as a child or adult, abused a position of power, even a little bit?

Have you ever been mean to someone you saw as a romantic rival?

Have you ever, as a child or adult, helped spread a nasty rumor about someone?

Have you ever, as a child or adult, wished someone harm?

Have you ever, as a child or adult, taken more than your share of something?

Have you ever, as a child or adult, taken/stolen anything you felt you deserved?

Is there anything that you could do that would make your life better that you are too afraid to do?

If you answered yes to any or all of these questions, congratulations, you are a human being. Remember that villains are not inhuman; they are humans who are ruled by these baser feelings and thoughts. All monsters in the living world and the story world are manifestations of these emotions. This includes trolls, dragons, witches, vampires, invaders from space, and evil kings. It includes Iago, Cinderella's wicked stepmother, Captain Ahab, the serpent in the Garden of Eden, Little Red Riding Hood's wolf, Captain Hook, Darth Vader, Dr. Hannibal Lecter, Ebenezer Scrooge, Professor Moriarty, Lex Luthor, Lady

MacBeth, and Beelzebub himself. But it also includes Tomás de Torquemada, Pol Pot, Joseph Stalin, Idi Amin, Heinrich Himmler, Caligula, Josef Mengele, Countess Elizabeth Báthory, Benito Mussolini, and the Rev. Jim Jones.

I'm not saying that there is no difference between villains who actually lived and murdered people and those who exist only in the world of story. What I am saying is that there is no difference in the traits they possess and that therefore the lesson for the audience is the same: do not behave as these people do, and watch out for these people in life.

In the case of villains, the Golden Theme is defined by its absence. Villains put themselves first at all times—they allow their baser instincts to take them over.

It is important for us storytellers to understand that if we create characters that are inhuman monsters, then we create two-dimensional caricatures that no one can relate to. No one views themselves as a monster, so there is no reason for the audience to look inside themselves and confront the Hitler there if they do not, on some level, identify with the villain of the story.

Mother Teresa's battle is one we all fight. The reason we are elated to see the hero win over evil is because the hero's struggle is our struggle.

As storytellers, we must also be careful not to make the hero too good. We all want to see ourselves as the hero, but if the hero of a story is too perfect, we cannot identify. The audience must be able to see that the hero has doubts and fears just as they do, and that the hero overcomes them. This is the Gorgon we must all defeat.

A hero or heroine must understand the Golden Theme and put her own or his own life in a secondary position to a greater good, just as the Hutu pastor who hid the women in his bathroom did.

Whenever possible, a storyteller should draw a parallel between the hero's weakness and the villain's. That way the audience can measure the triumph of the hero against the failure of the villain with a direct comparison.

When there is victory over evil in a story we are invested in, there is a sense of catharsis.

This catharsis can also come with a tragic ending. But connecting with another person on an emotional level, a level beyond words, is transcendent. The ancient Greeks believed that this feeling was medicinal. It is the feeling we get when we understand the Golden Theme.

As storytellers we must find the part of villains that is like ourselves, as this will give them depth.

SAINTLY HEROES AND
THE GOLDEN THEME

A man does not have to be an angel in order to be a saint.

—Albert Schweitzer

I want to address the hero I warned you about earlier—the hero who is too good. If you write about these characters, you must understand their effect.

When a hero is flawless, or virtually flawless, people often feel a sense of distance from that hero. Superman is an example of this kind of hero—too good to be real. And yet he is the king of all superheroes. This is because we see this kind of character as an ideal more than a character. They are, for want of a better term, saints. These people or characters live the Golden Theme by putting others first—always. They will risk or give anything in service to others, including their very lives.

Or they have a wellspring of compassion and understanding even for those who would do them harm, or have done them harm. Anne Frank was a girl who, along with her family and four others, hid for two years from the Nazis during World War II but was eventually betrayed, arrested, and sent to Bergen-Belsen concentration camp, where she died of typhus.

Despite all she had been through, she was able to write these famous words in her diary:

"It's really a wonder that I haven't dropped all my ideals, because they seem so absurd and impossible to carry out. Yet I keep them, because in spite of everything I still believe that people are really good at heart."

This ability to see the good in people when there is so much evidence to the contrary is nothing short of superhuman. The people with this kind of love for humanity are seen by us as the godliest among us—or even as God.

When a woman was brought before Jesus to be stoned

to death because she had committed the sin of adultery, his words were a version of the Golden Theme: "Let him who is without sin cast the first stone." This is a man many believe to be God. And even of those who do not, few will deny his godliness. This act of compassion is the physical manifestation of the Golden Theme.

I will not attempt to say this better than Buddha, who said, "The practice of making others happy is based upon the clear understanding of life which is Oneness. In deep gratitude, let us realize this Oneness of all life, the heart of which is Compassion."

If you choose to write one of these characters, you must give them big obstacles to overcome. It must be one person, armed only with the truth, against an entire government. Or they must have their philosophy of life challenged to the point where they are tempted to throw it all away. Even these people must have a vulnerable spot. This is so we can see ourselves in them. If we can see ourselves, then we can attempt to live up to these figures.

I do not want to trivialize the work and lives of real people whom I admire by once again bringing up Superman. But in the end, this person who occupies the story world still represents what we think is good in the world. But even Superman has his kryptonite. It is important that a character so powerful have something that could kill him—so that he can risk his life to save others. This way he can show selflessness. Here is someone with great powers who uses them not for himself, but for a greater good. We would all like to live in a world where power is used to help and not hurt. Just like all story heroes and heroes in life, Superman shows us who we can be.

It has been revealed that even Mother Teresa, a woman who dedicated her life to helping people, feared being perceived as a hypocrite because she had deep doubts about her faith. In the book *Mother Teresa: Come Be My Light,* co-written with Brian Kolodiejchuk, she wrote, "Where is my faith? ... there is nothing but emptiness and darkness... If there be God— please forgive me."

Her words are not unlike the words of Jesus, the God she worshiped, as he suffered on the cross. From the Book of Matthew: "And about the ninth hour Jesus cried with a loud voice, saying, "My God, my God why hast thou forsaken me?"

The struggles of a hero must be tremendous. We measure the merit of heroes based on their struggles and sacrifices. This tells us that it is never easy to be a good person. It tells us that it is as hard for them as it would be for any of us, and knowing this we marvel at those who choose this way of life—and sometimes this way of death.

If you choose to tell stories about these people, remember that they, too, are like us and have their weaknesses, and that showing these weaknesses only reveals how strong they really are.

Remember, the nutrient of a story is the survival information contained within. We are not just speaking of the survival of individuals, but the survival of humanity. Sometimes that requires some of us to make great sacrifices. It requires the belief that another's life is as precious, or more precious, than our own. Stories teach this lesson again and again.

If a character lives the Golden Theme completely, they will be seen as saintly or godlike figures and must be given challenges to match.

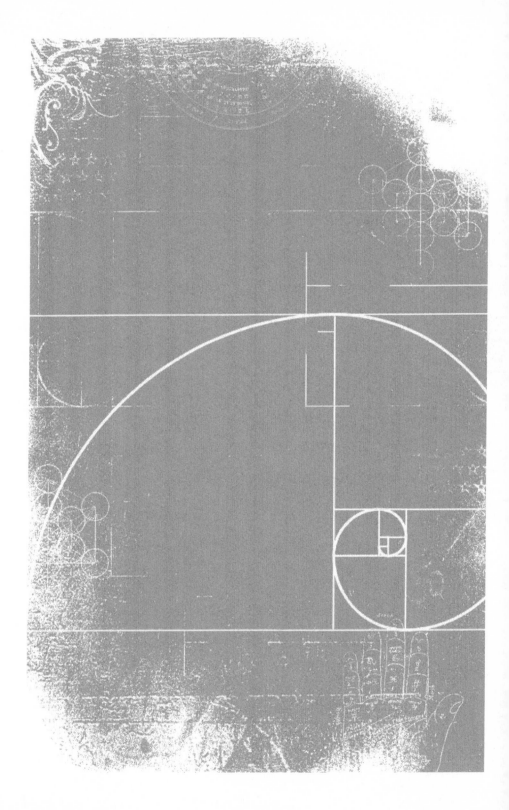

····· STYLE AND THE GOLDEN THEME ·····

Showing off is the fool's idea of glory.

—Bruce Lee

Style for style's sake is the goal of the amateur artist or storyteller. This is ego-based storytelling.

Young or inexperienced artists are very concerned with style and in recent years, their teachers have been telling them to find their style, their voice. They do not say to them, "Learn the craft of storytelling." Instead, they say, "Find your voice." This goal of finding one's voice is in direct conflict with the Golden Theme because it is a selfish goal. It comes out of a desire to be noticed.

It is showing off.

Think of it this way: would you feel safer crossing a high bridge where the designer was more concerned with the color of the paint than structural integrity? Or maybe you would like your surgery to be performed by a doctor who handled his instruments with flair? In these cases, emphasis on style seems ridiculous, doesn't it? If stories are for our survival, if they are medicine, then they cannot be about the storyteller. As a storyteller, you are a servant of your story, not the master. You must do what it requires, not what you want it to do. You must remove your ego from it. Art is not to show people who you are; it is to show people who they are. Or to put it more accurately, it is to show us who we are—as human beings.

Telling an artist to express himself or herself only produces self-indulgent, mediocre art.

A better way to say it might be to tell artists to expose themselves. If an artist digs deep inside, reveals the deepest parts of himself, and exposes it to the world, the artist will disappear and the audience will only see themselves. To do this properly, one must strip away all style. It only clouds your point.

A great painter does not paint things differently; he sees

things differently. He is only painting the truth as he sees it. Your job as a storyteller is to tell the truth—the deep truth—the truth as you see it. If you do this even while trying not to have a style, you will have one. Style is what happens as a result of how you solve a given problem.

Legendary comic book storyteller Will Eisner put it this way: "Technique is secondary. Technique comes as a result of *how* you do *what* you do."

The other reason people concentrate on style is lack of confidence. It is a diversion—a misdirection. It is a way of saying *notice* me, but please don't *see* me. It is trying hard to dazzle people with style so that the focus is taken off real intrinsic problems. This makes as much sense as trying to cure cancer with a nice new suit. The patient may look better, but he is still ill.

The irony is that if you forget about being noticed, take your ego out of your work, and express the Golden Theme as purely as you can, you stand a greater chance of being noticed. But more importantly, you will reach people—move them. And when people comment on your style, you will have no idea what they are talking about because your work will penetrate so much further below the surface that style will become unimportant to you.

Critics love style and write about it incessantly. However, if you focus on it you may go far, but you'll never go deep.

Style is ego-based and is in direct conflict with the Golden Theme.

DIVERSITY AND THE GOLDEN THEME

There are not many but only One. Who sees variety and not unity wanders from death to death.

—The Upanishads

In recent years, we have begun to talk an awful lot about diversity and the celebration of it. I believe our focus has been in the wrong place. Stories have taught me that our differences are unimportant. It's not important what we eat; it's important that we eat. It's not important whom we love; it's only important that we love. It's not important what music we enjoy; it's just important that we enjoy music. It's not important how we grieve; it's important that we grieve. It is only important that we all laugh, and that we all cry. A person in China gets no hungrier than a person in Africa. A mother in New York worries no more for her children than a mother in Mexico.

These are the things that connect us all, and if we learn this, our differences will fall away and disappear. We would do far better celebrating our sameness.

Does this mean that your stories cannot make use of your culture? No, the culture will give the story richness, but where an outsider will connect with the story is on the most basic human level. Speak to all human beings when you tell stories. If you do this, what will happen is what happens with animal stories—they will see themselves more clearly because distance provides perspective. You will reveal them to themselves. They will see the Golden Theme more clearly.

A few years ago, I made a short film called *White Face*. The film did very well. It won some awards and has had a long life, which is unusual for a short film. It has been seen all over the world. It is now used for diversity training at various companies.

The film is a fake documentary about the problems clowns would have if they were an actual race of people.

Over the years, I have gotten many compliments on the film, but none as great as the one I am about to share with you.

One day, I received a call from an organization that wanted me to come and show the film and do a Q & A. While I was on the phone, the man who called went on about how much he liked the film. He was reciting lines back to me and laughing. Then he said that he wanted to tell me a story.

He said that a woman he knew was upset because her daughter was going to marry a black man. The entire family was quite distraught over this. He told her he had a film she should see and gave her *White Face*. After she and her husband watched it, they realized just how ridiculous they had been and decided to welcome this man into their family.

That was the best compliment I have ever gotten about the film because what it says is that, after seeing it, they understood the Golden Theme.

I treated everything in the film as if it were real. I used real problems to inform the problems of the Clown race. And although there are laughs in the film, nothing was played for laughs.

This story world provided this woman and her husband the opportunity to see themselves at a distance—it gave them perspective. Think about this for a second. These were people old enough to have an adult daughter. Surely they had been told that their views were wrong. They had probably heard it all their lives. But in those cases, they were being scolded or preached to.

In this case, they were just watching a story and saw themselves. It healed them. Now we are back to stories as medicine.

I take no credit for this; it is the Golden Theme at work. If you adhere to it, you may change lives.

Focusing on differences instead of similarities blinds us to the Golden Theme.

Origin Stories and
the Golden Theme

The universe is made of stories, not atoms.

—Muriel Rukeyser

Origin stories are very important to human beings and are among the most sacred. The story of how a family came to live in America, for instance. *My grandparents came here with nothing*, it might begin. These types of stories are precious to us. So it makes sense that we are so adamant about the ones we believe in.

Scientists tell us the universe was once contained in a very small point called a *singularity*. This point exploded and expanded, becoming the universe. Inside this singularity was everything that makes up the universe—everything. Every star, every nebula, every particle of matter was in that small, infinitely dense singularity. This includes everything that makes us up as well. This means that we are literally all made of the same stuff.

The biblical story tells us that we are all descended from two people called Adam and Eve. There again, we are all related.

In America, we are obsessed with race, but scientists tell us that there is no such thing.

They say that our cosmetic differences are just that. Genetically we, as individuals, might share more in common with a member of another race than someone of our own. Archaeological and genetic data shows that early modern humans migrated out of East Africa and spread to the rest of the globe. They say too that it was a relatively small group that left Africa.

I include this short chapter only to point out that contained within all our stories and contained within our very DNA is the message that we are all the same. Science is only confirming what we must already understand.

Our origin stories, from science to religion, tell us that we are all the same.

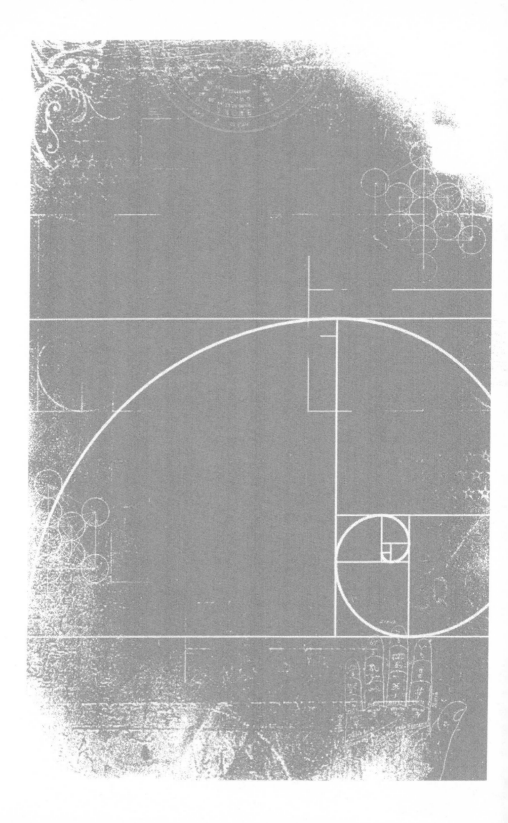

A QUICK LESSON IN APPLYING
THE GOLDEN THEME

An individual has not started living until he can rise above the narrow confines of his individualistic concerns to the broader concerns of all humanity.

— Martin Luther King, Jr.

A good friend of mine is a photojournalist and at one time was a photo editor at a newspaper.

One day, we were discussing storytelling in our respective fields. He was talking about the importance of photo layout. His example was a hypothetical story about an impoverished village in Africa where the people had to walk five miles each day to get fresh water. He said that many editors would go for the shots of hungry children to try to create empathy. He said that wasn't the best way to build a connection with the audience, that the way to get people to engage was to have some pictures of hungry children and at least one or two that showed universal activities.

For instance, a picture of a father helping a child tie her shoe before they went on their walk.

Then readers could see scenes that they were familiar with. Maybe they have kids and have done this themselves. Or, at the very least, they have been children who needed help tying their shoes.

Now people can imagine themselves in the situation and will have deeper feelings about what they see.

When I told him about the Golden Theme he said that he would have had an easier time explaining things to his photographers if he had known to say, *Find a way that shows we are all the same.* This is what you need to do.

In the Pixar film *The Incredibles*, a story about a family of superheroes, the creators were always sure to contrast something fantastic against something very human. They were a superhero family with real-world problems. The middle-aged father has a paunch, for instance.

Or the children use their superpowers at the dinner

table while having an otherwise normal brother/sister argument. This makes the story accessible. Find ways to let people into your story.

The more you do this, the greater your connection to your audience. And the more you will be stating the Golden Theme.

Using the Golden Theme helps people identify with the stories you tell them.

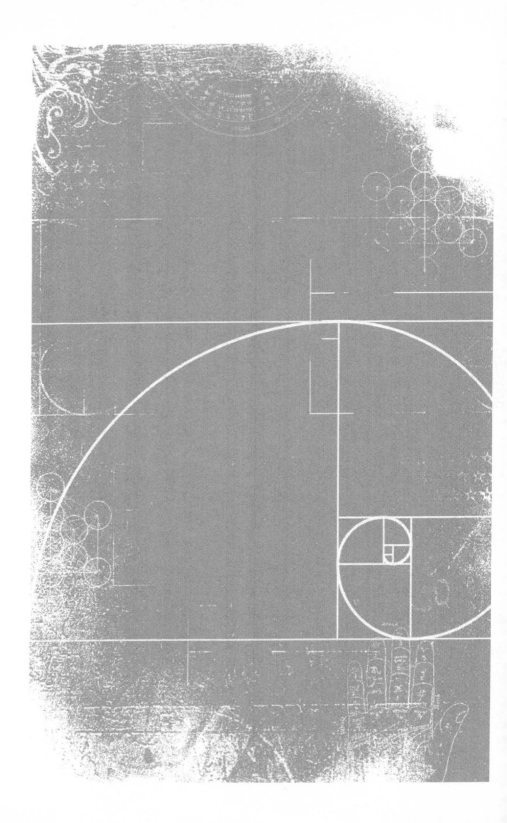

CHARACTER CHANGE AND
THE GOLDEN THEME

············

The only way I know of bringing about better understanding between different peoples is to treat all as of ourselves.

—Mahatma Gandhi

One of the most practical uses of the Golden Theme for a storyteller is taking a character from no knowledge, or denial of the concept, to complete understanding of it.

Mark Twain was a celebrated writer before he wrote *The Adventures of Huckleberry Finn,* so why is it considered his masterpiece? It is because, at its core, it says that we are all the same.

Huck Finn is a boy, not unlike Twain himself, who grew up in a world of slavery. But Huck finds himself running away from his life along with a slave named Jim, who is running to freedom. On their journey, Huck overhears Jim, whom he is becoming fond of, crying for the family he has left behind. It is a revelation to the boy that a black man would mourn the loss of his family the same as a white one would. Huck is beginning to understand the Golden Theme.

Huck has been taught that helping a slave escape is not just a crime but also a sin—a sin that carries with it eternal damnation. And still when he could turn him in, he doesn't. He'd rather go to Hell than deny that Jim is just as human as he is and deserves to be free by virtue of that humanity. Sacrifice is the ultimate expression of the Golden Theme.

In real life, this knowledge also has a powerful effect and can change people deeply.

Let's take something very close to what happened to Huck.

Charles Black was a white civil rights lawyer who worked on the landmark case to desegregate public schools in the American South. But he started out life having no knowledge of the Golden Theme. All that changed in 1931 when he heard Louis Armstrong play the trumpet.

He heard genius where he was taught there was none. "It is impossible to overstate the significance of a sixteen-year-old Southern boy's seeing genius, for the first time, in a black," he said later in the *Yale Law Journal*. This made him question all that he had been taught. Black now saw segregation as "that most hideous of errors," and said it was "the failure to recognize kinship." It transformed him. He knew that we are all the same.

Civil rights leader Malcolm X is a controversial figure because he was once a member of the Nation of Islam, or the black Muslims. The Nation of Islam preached that white people were devils, and Malcolm believed this and preached it himself.

Let's look at Malcolm's life. He was a black man, born in America in the 1920s. His father was killed by the Ku Klux Klan. He was a good student and graduated at the top of his junior high class. But when he told his favorite teacher he wanted to be a lawyer, he was told that was "no realistic goal for a nigger." Years later, when he was in prison for robbery, he was introduced to the Nation of Islam and taught that all white men were devils. It made sense to him. He had no evidence to the contrary.

As is required of all Muslims, he went on a pilgrimage to Mecca. Here he found something he didn't expect—he met white Muslims. He said he met, "blond-haired, blued-eyed men I could call my brothers." When he came back to America, he no longer talked of separatism but of unity. He had learned the Golden Theme. Malcolm is still a controversial figure because of his "white devil" statements, but he should be remembered as a man who saw, at last, that we are all the same.

John Newton was a slave ship captain who came to realize that trafficking in human beings was a crime against humanity. Newton went from one end of the Golden Theme to the other. So changed was he by this awakening that he wrote the enduring hymn, Amazing Grace. His lyrics are a testament to the power of understanding the Golden Theme:

> *Amazing grace! (how sweet the sound)*
> *That sav'd a wretch like me!*
> *I once was lost, but now am found,*
> *Was blind, but now I see.*

Oskar Schindler was a German war profiteer who used Jewish slave labor during World War II. After seeing the violent raid on the Krakow Ghetto, where Jews were rounded up by soldiers to be shipped off to concentration camps, Schindler began to recognize the humanity of the people he was exploiting. After that, he went to work saving the Jews under his employ. He even brought in more workers to be saved. He saved some 1,200 Jews from almost certain death.

Of course people can, and do, go the other way. They can start off having more empathy and become hard and bitter. Aristotle says that the best stories depict people better than average or worse than average. The former would include those discussed earlier in this chapter—those who accept the Golden Theme. Conversely, the worse than average are those who reject it.

For instance, let's say that Charles Black, who was stunned by Louis Armstrong's genius, had gone the other way. What if he was a struggling trumpet player who was shamed by seeing a black man who played better than he? It could have happened that way. He could have decided to tighten segregation. He could have fought to suppress such genius to try and hide his own inadequacies. In story terms, he then becomes an antihero.

This kind of story is just as worth telling because it still expresses the Golden Theme through the lack of it. It tells us who not to be. It is just as important to know who not to be as who to be.

A character who goes from one end of understanding the Golden Theme to the other is compelling and makes for good storytelling.

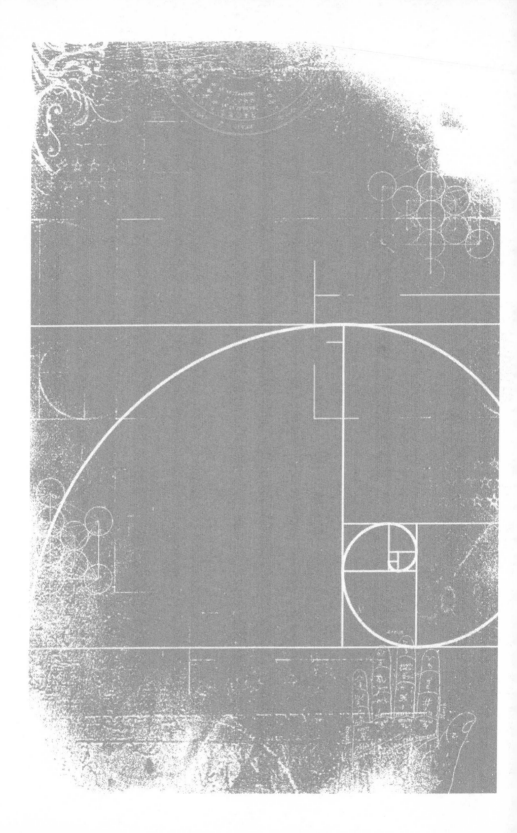

THE LAND OF THE DEAD AND THE GOLDEN THEME

Love the beings of the world equally and universally. The Universe is One.

—Chuang-tzu

My father died a few months ago. One of the things it does to us when someone close to us dies is cause us to look at our own lives and eventual deaths. If the Golden Theme is true, you are thinking of it even as you read these words. In addition to my father, one of my best friends died a few years ago, and I would be lying if I said that I didn't think of my own death despite wanting to focus on my father and friend.

It so happens that I have been reading the ancient Sumerian *Epic of Gilgamesh*, which is at least 3,500 years old and is the oldest collection of stories we know of. In the story, Gilgamesh's best friend, Enkidu, dies. His first response is disbelief. He thinks that if he grieves hard enough, his friend may come back to life. Consumed by grief, he doesn't even bother to bathe. He wants the whole world to stop and mourn the death of his friend.

When Gilgamesh understands that Enkidu is not coming back from the dead he comes to realize that he, too, will one day die.

This story was told thousands of years before I was born and yet the teller understands what I am feeling. The story easily crosses time, language, and culture to tell me that I am not alone. It tells me that others have felt as I do right now. It comforts me. As I said before, the truth can't tell time.

After his realization, Gilgamesh goes on a journey to seek eternal life. On his journey, he must cross the Waters of Death. When he reaches his destination, he is told that death is necessary and all things end, and that he should enjoy his life because death eventually comes to us all.

There are many stories where characters journey to the

Land of the Dead to gain wisdom.

The Land of the Dead, as I define it, is a place where there is actual death or the very real possibility of death. It might be a place where it is a struggle to survive from one day to the next.

It may be a place where people are in serious mental or physical pain. It can be a place where great suffering has happened or is happening.

In the case of Gilgamesh, it was the Waters of Death. There is great wisdom in the Land of the Dead. People in the living world and people in the story world learn a lot when they take that journey.

In the story of the Buddha's early life, it is said that he was a prince named Siddhartha who lived in a palace where his father, who wanted him to be a great king, shielded him from all knowledge of human suffering.

The king saw to it that his son wanted for nothing, but Siddhartha felt that there must be more to life than wealth. One day the young prince left the palace to meet his subjects. For 29 years, he had been shielded from the world. While out among the people Siddhartha saw, for the first time in his life, an old man and this sight disturbed him.

He was then told by his chariot driver that one day we

all grow old and die. On subsequent explorations the prince encountered, among other distressing things, the decaying body of a dead man. After realizing the suffering that life contains, he strove to overcome decrepitude, disease and death by living a life free of indulgences.

This is the story of the beginning of Siddhartha's path to enlightenment — the path to becoming the Buddha. Siddhartha's journey into the world was also his journey into the Land of the Dead.

There is a Mongolian folktale that takes place at the time of a great plague that killed both young and old. Death from this sickness was quick but painful.

A young boy named Tarvaa took sick and lingered for days; weak from fever, he lost all awareness of the living world. And thinking he was dead, Tarvaa's spirit left his body and journeyed to the Underworld.

Once in the Underworld he was greeted by its Great Khan, who asked the boy why he had left his body before it had died. The boy explained that his family had stood around him, sure that he would perish, and rather than suffer any longer, he left his body to come to the Underworld.

The Khan told Tarvaa that it was not yet his time and that he had to return the world. But the Khan was touched by the boy, and told him that he could choose any gift in the Underworld to take with him.

When the boy looked around he saw that everything one could imagine among the treasures of life — every pleasure and pain that existed. Fine clothes, good food, music, good luck and bad, wealth and poverty, dance, laughter, sadness and many other temptations both good and bad were there.

He pointed to the one thing he wanted. The Khan nodded kindly and told the boy to return to the world of the living and to use his gift well on the earth. The boy had chosen storytelling. This is how storytelling came to be.

Tarvaa kept his promise to the Great Khan and used his gift well. He traveled far and wide telling and collecting stories and became the greatest storyteller in all of Mongolia.

Here too all of the wisdom comes from the Land of the Dead. For Mongolians, stories themselves are from the Underworld.

In the classic action film *Raiders of the Lost Ark* the hero, Indiana Jones, is searching for the biblical Ark of the Covenant and must descend into The Well of Souls, which is depicted as a tomb. He is even greeted, upon opening the tomb, by a statue with the head of a jackal.

This is Anubis the Egyptian God of the Dead. Indiana Jones must enter The Land of the Dead to obtain what he seeks.

On a more serious note one of my first students was a breast cancer survivor. She had faced death and decided that when she was well, she would change her life—and she did. She quit her job to pursue becoming a writer. She learned the same lesson as Gilgamesh: that she should enjoy her life because death comes to us all.

People who have been in terrible wars often have a profound understanding of the Golden Theme. They see that life and death can have a kind of randomness that is unsettling. We go through much of our early life believing that we are a little special and death will probably pass us by. But when you understand that death can happen to anyone at any time, you understand that we are all the same.

Anne Frank lived in the Land of the Dead and gained great wisdom there. Wisdom often comes at a great cost. We owe it to her to listen to what she learned.

Albert Schweitzer and Mother Teresa lived in the Land of the Dead and both have much to tell us. What is a slave ship if not the Land of the Dead? John Newton learned so much there that his transformative grief echoes across time through his famous hymn healing those who feel a kinship with the long-dead ship's captain. Oskar Schindler was compelled to save lives after his journey to the Land of the Dead. The further one goes into the Land of the Dead, the bigger the lessons to be learned. Stories are a way for us to gain this wisdom without having to visit the Land of the Dead ourselves. Or they can teach us what to do when we find ourselves there.

Stories need conflict because no one needs to know how to get along when things are going well. It's the bad times that teach us how to survive in life and in stories. The Land of the Dead is a place of much conflict. Big conflict, big lesson.

The woman who visited the cemetery because her son was dying was visiting the Land of the Dead for comfort. The dead there told her that she was not alone.

Years ago, when I was walking through that cemetery with my friend and wondered aloud what all of those dead people would say if they could talk, I assumed that it was a question that could never be answered. I was wrong.

We have a saying, "Silent as the grave." But graveyards are not silent at all. Every headstone there is saying one thing and saying it loudly to anyone who takes the time to listen. They are saying, "We are all the same."

Stories are the collective wisdom of everyone who has ever lived. Your job as a storyteller is not simply to entertain. Nor is it to be noticed for the way you turn a phrase. You have a very important job—one of the most important. Your job is to let people know that everyone shares their feelings—and that these feelings bind us. Your job is a healing art, and like all healers, you have a responsibility. Let people know that they are not alone. You must make people understand that we are all the same.

GREAT READS FROM TALKING DRUM, LLC

Invisible Ink **by Brian McDonald**   Invisible Ink teaches the essential elements of the best storytelling from award-winning writer/director/producer Brian McDonald.

Ink Spots **by Brian McDonald**   Ink Spots is a collection of essays on writing, story structure and filmmaking by award-winning writer/director/producer Brian McDonald.

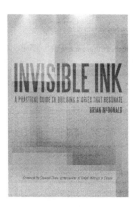
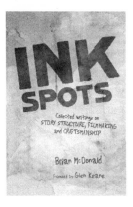

Made in the USA
Middletown, DE
19 June 2017